ADVENTURES OF TIMMY & BEVY

Superhero's

BEVERLEY ROSE LYNN THOMSON

BEVERLEY ROSE LYNN THOMSON

Draw your family picture above.

ADVENTURES OF TIMMY & BEVY

Copyright © 2023 Beverley Rose Lynn Thomson

All rights reserved. This book or any portion thereof may not be reproduced or used in any manner whatsoever without the express written permission of the publisher except for use of brief quotations in a book review. It is not legal to reproduce, duplicate, or transmit any part of this document in either electronic means or printed format. Recording of this publication is strictly prohibited.

You can reach Beverley through her website https://beverleythomson.com/

ISBN: 9798391375241

ADVENTURES OF TIMMY & BEVY

DEDICATION

To a wonderful brother, friend and mentor, Tim (Timmy) Thomson.

To Scotia and Briar

who loves listening to our childhood bedtime stories.

REVIEWS

★★★★★ We read this story with the children 6-10. The children enjoyed hearing the adventures of Bevy and Timmy. They loved all the animals in the story, and it started a good conversation about their pets. They laughed at the funny things that happened along the way. Tammy Jaipaul, RECE, Evangel Day Care

★★★★★The children enjoyed listening to all the adventures, and the excitement the children had in this book. They related things in their live to the story. "I went to Sauble Beach before".   Evangel Day Care

"We loved reading this story" -so funny. Children at the Evangel Daycare.

★★★★★ Wonderful and uplifting experience reading this book, following the adventures of Bev and Tim, brother and sister as they encounter many changes in their lives

What stood out for me was how these changes and at times, life threatening moments, were less scary, more joyous, and less overwhelming because they had each other. So much inspiration and being a Registered Therapist, I would definitely encourage my clients to read this book to explore the importance and power of having someone with you during both the challenges and adventures in our lives. Chris Werbski MSW, RSW, RP

★★★★★ "I think this book is great and children and parents will enjoy reading it. I loved all the little mini stories and it reminded me of how it was so very different growing up than it is now. Reminded me of all the adventures and trouble I would get into with my baby sister." Dr. Kiran Gosal, MSc, DDS.

CONTENTS

	Dedication & Reviews	i
1	Cuddles	1
2	Tommy The Turtle	Pg #3
3	Time To Fly	Pg #5
4	Saving Kittens	Pg #7
5	Auction Day	Pg #9
6	The Halloween Party	Pg #11
7	Christmas Cookies	Pg #13
8	New Friends	Pg #15
9	Apple Picking	Pg #17
10	The Silver Bus	Pg #19
11	Our Dog Candy	Pg #21
12	Snuggles	Pg #23
10	Illustrator	Pg #27
11	Editors	Pg #29
12	Author	Pg #30

ADVENTURES OF TIMMY & BEVY

INTRODUCTION

A children's book created from real life experiences of a brother and sister and their fun adventures with parents that moved around a lot in the 1970's. Adults like reminiscing while reading; while children wait with anticipation for the next adventure. This book will show your children how much fun they can have playing outside. Below Bevy & Timmy today and as children.

1 CUDDLES

I jumped out of my bed and wandered into my brother's room thinking, "Where had the little fellow gone?" Mommy was crying in the kitchen and seemed very sad. Why, wasn't anyone telling me what was going on? All of a sudden, Daddy grabbed me, and took me for a ride in the car and explained that we were on our way to sneak me into the hospital to visit "little Timmy" who was really sick. I felt like a superhero going to save my brother.

We bypassed the reception and sneaked by the nurses. My dad, running with me in his arms, we landed in a white room with my little brother lying in a tiny steel bed surrounded by plastic within a bubble. Timmy was hooked up to all these tubes and wires, and I felt afraid for him. Daddy said, "Bevy, you need to go hug little Timmy, he needs you." Then without any delay, I found myself in Dad's big arms, being huddled into Timmy's bed, beneath his blankets, under the bubble. I grabbed my brother tightly, and gave him the biggest hug in the world. We both fell into a deep sleep snuggled up tightly together, holding on for dear life.

It must be morning; the bright sun came shining in on our faces and the nurse spoke up and shouted, "What are you doing in here?" My daddy said to the nurse, "Timmy just needed his sister's love last night." I woke up laughing and kissing my little brother's cute face, and to my surprise, he was all better, and the nurse said he could probably go home today. The doctors and nurses rushed into the room. "It was a miracle, who was this little girl in bed with this dying child?" "What? (I shouted) I was his big sister, and he was my little brother and we're going home today!" Daddy later said I had saved his life and that all Timmy needed was a big hug to make him all better. It was then I realized that I had been rewarded with the greatest gift of my life - a little brother whom I could love for the rest of my life - Timmy!

2 TOMMY THE TURTLE

Kindergarten was fun, painting, colouring, meeting new friends. Wow, Daddy showed up at school to give Timmy and me a ride home. He had a pet turtle that was coming to live with us. We jumped into the car with excitement – petting our new friend's long neck and hard shell. We called him Tommy the Turtle. Tommy was to live in our bathtub with rocks and a little water. Mommy, didn't like Tommy living in the bathtub so she said he should live outside and he would have more fun. Daddy took us to the pet store to buy Tommy turtle food.

We asked Daddy for a pool to put Tommy in, so daddy built us an outdoor circular pool around the willow tree. Timmy and I had so much fun swimming in our new pool, and it was hard to share it with Tommy. We lived in Keswick close to the beach – so my thinking was that Tommy could walk to the beach if he wanted a swim. All of a sudden Timmy and I had lots of friends because we had a turtle and a pool. That was kind of cool! I started thinking I should do what mommy does when she has company. So I started baking cookies for everyone in the neighborhood, but Timmy was to try them first. I went digging for sand, dirt, leaves, stones and a board and started preparing my dirt cookies, cakes sprinkled with sand, and specialty dishes.

Mommy started wondering why Timmy was not eating dinner. I told her it was all the stones that he was sucking the dirt off to taste my delectable cookies. Oh boy I got sent to my room and told that daddy was going to buy me an Easy Bake Oven instead. So then Timmy got candies, cakes and cookies fresh from my toy oven. He liked them more than the dirt cookies and they didn't make him sick. Daddy said I might want to become a chef when I grow up.

3 TIME TO FLY

We moved to a townhouse in Brampton, and I thought it was time for Timmy to learn to fly like the birds outside, so I took my little brother out to the biggest rock I could find and told him to flap his arms until he flew. Timmy looked scared and didn't want to fly. I told him just flap your arms and you will fly like Fuzzy the fly that flew around the house. Still, he seemed to need a push. Poor little Timmy ended up in a hospital with a cast because he couldn't flap hard enough. I guess Timmy couldn't fly but at least he tried, and I felt it my job as his big sister to try to teach him.

There was a new shopping mall being built across the street. That meant we had tunnels to play in and new paths to ride our bikes in. Mommy and daddy just told us to go out and play, so play we did. We met new kids and even jumped on a local bus and went for a tour of Brampton until the bus driver took us home.

Daddy said we needed to stay busy at home so we helped him build a new kind of tent. This was fun making tents in the basement and testing tents on the front lawn. My best friend, Heather, came over and we spent the night in daddy's new tent on the front lawn. Timmy was our security guard.

The next day, Daddy showed up at our school and told us he had a surprise and asked Timmy if he wanted the present inside the house or outside. Tim took inside and I took outside. Tim's present was a new sauna Dad had built and was starting to sell. That was kinda cool! But my gift was even better. I got a new wooden swing set in the back yard wrapped in a gigantic yellow bow and Timmy loved it too. We both shared our gifts and felt like we had the richest parents in the world buying us these amazing gifts. Just when life was great, our parents told us were moving again from Brampton to a farm not far away.

4 SAVING KITTENS

Mommy and Daddy packed up all our toys and clothes and we were moving outside Brampton. Daddy had just purchased a farm for us to live in; with a tree house, and fancy fruit trees. Timmy and I decided to go down the road over the bridge to the river and swim in the cool water while the cars drove overhead. All of a sudden, a potato sack fell on Timmy's head – a car must have driven past and dropped the bag into the river. Inquisitively, we quickly untied the rope around the sack. All of a sudden, we heard little sounds and whispers coming from the bag. The knot was tight. I grabbed a sharp rock and together with my brother, Timmy, we worked quickly to open the potato sack. To our surprise seven little kittens were in the sack! Wow! They were so cute, so we took the sack of kittens back to our new farm to live in the barn and roam free and chase the mice.

Timmy and I, were both so excited we ran into the house and pulled the milk jug out of the fridge pouring the kittens milk, and then set them free in the barn to roam. Over the next few weeks, the group of seven grew and caught mice, found food, and played with us every day. Mommy seemed a little perturbed that we had brought the kittens' home; but daddy just thought it was great and the kittens just followed us everywhere down the lane, into the barn, and into the forest area at the back.

At night time, we rounded up the kittens and snuck them into our bed and played with them until we all fell asleep. During the day they would run up the tree into our treehouse and play house with us. One of the kittens caught a mouse we named Sammy, so Timmy put it in a cage and kept it as his new pet. For some reason mommy didn't like Sammy but we loved him and daddy took us to the pet store to buy him food. Now we had a mouse, seven cats and a great new tree house. We were so happy!

5 AUCTION DAY

Today was auction day, and we were hoping to see Wilbur, Charlotte's friend, or the cat in the hat with the red striped hat at the farm auction. Instead, Daddy found us two new ponies to bring home – one for me and one for Timmy. Our ponies lived in the apple orchard and we shared our apples with them. I was kind of happy I didn't have to share our cherries from the tree as I loved them and they tasted so good right off the tree. One pony was for me and the big one for Timmy. My little pony was fun and liked it when I jumped on her and she took me for rides around the orchard. My brother's pony was not so social, because he liked to run free on his own with the wind in his face. When I jumped on my pony for a ride, I could reach the apples and get a ride to the school bus every day at the end of the driveway. How much better could our lives get?

Daddy took us back again to the auction and this time we bought twelve baby chicks. Daddy bought an incubator for the babies to keep them warm. Pretty soon we had lots of chickens and mom used some of the fresh farm eggs every day for breakfast. One of the chickens used to chase Timmy around the farm and peck at his shoes, and it was funny to watch. Timmy didn't have much luck with birds because outside we had two wild geese in our driveway that loved to chase him. They must have decided to live with us on the farm. They were bigger than us and would bite Timmy. Mommy said they were "wild" geese and wild animals are not the same as pet animals, and that's why they would chase us away from the barn. Even though it was funny watching the wild geese chase my little brother up and down the driveway, we had to make a new path to get to the chickens so the geese wouldn't catch us. Soon we learned to outsmart them, or watch them from one of the barn roofs.

Okay this is addictive, but back to the auction again! This time to pick up a cow! Daddy bid on a small baby calf that we called 'Blue' because he liked blue cold water. Blue roamed free, and came into the kitchen and helped himself to his bowl of water on the floor. It was like having a gigantic dog that came into the house and sat at the table with us eating and drinking milk and water. Mommy would feed Blue from a bottle filled with milk and was teaching him to drink from his bowl. He was so cute and let us pet him. Our new farm was so exciting, and we had so many animals to play with. Sometimes Mommy made the cow leave while we ate dinner. Blue would just go outside and eat the grass. Dad said Blue was helping us to look after the lawn.

6 THE HALLOWEEN PARTY

Dad fixed up our tree house and made it bigger for our tea parties. We could see all the farm pets (cats, chickens, geese, ponies, and cow) from up in our tree house and hide from our parents. Our parents and animals couldn't climb up the tree, so we had a new hiding spot 😊.

Halloween was coming and Dad said we were having a huge party and inviting all our neighbors. Dad built a rollercoaster through the barns and put up a scary fake ghost, cob webs and pumpkins. Timmy and I got to carve the pumpkin's face and put the candles in it to glow during the party. Blue dressed up and roamed around the party, and our horses put on fake horns to look scary for Halloween.

We invited all our friends and their parents and hid treats for the kids to try to find in the haystacks. It was so much fun! We had monster music and goblin cupcakes (I was not allowed to bake for this one) and hot dogs with red ketchup that looked like fake blood, to make our food look scary. Dad dressed up like a mummy and jumped up and out and scared us all. My friends said it was the best Halloween party they had ever been to. I loved Halloween, dressing up, laughing with friends and pretending to be scared.

7 CHRISTMAS COOKIES

Christmas was coming and it was time to chop down a tree and decorate it for all our presents. Timmy and I noticed a lot of gifts accumulating around the tree. We thought it was time to open a few gifts and play with them ahead of time, so we found some tape and opened a couple of swords and had a play fight. The hard thing was re-wrapping them so Santa wouldn't find out. But not before we had our sword fight. We had the greatest gift of all – plastic swords to fight each other and battle to the floor. Timmy would always lose and fall to the ground crying from pain while laughing his head off.

Mommy bought us Advent calendars to hang on the wall so you could count the days until Christmas. It was hard not to eat the chocolate ahead of time. We could smell the pine tree and the cookies baking in the oven. Blue loved sleeping next to the door and stealing a cookie every time Mom's head was turned. We learned from him and tried it too, but we got caught and were sent to our rooms. If only Blue could bring us some cookies too! Oh well, we snuck a couple of kittens in to sleep with us under the covers.

On Christmas eve, we left out cookies and milk for Santa. This worked because when we woke up, we noticed more presents around the tree than the night before. When Christmas day arrived, Timmy and I acted like we had just seen the swords for the first time, but by this time we were pros and started fighting each other until one person fell to the ground laughing. Mommy cooked a big turkey dinner for our friends and relatives. Everyone got so full they all went to rest after dinner, while Timmy and I battled it out with our new swords.

8 NEW FRIENDS

Mommy and daddy started taking us to play at other kids' houses near ours. This was interesting and fun meeting new families and friends. One family lived in a subdivision and they hung out in a gang of four kids and played outdoor games we never heard of. One of the games was nicky nicky nine doors. When it's your turn we all go up to a door and one person has to knock and wait to the count of five and then we all run before the stranger answers the door. It was so much fun until one of the neighbours told our parents and again, we got sent to our rooms. Man, it's hard being a kid, learning what is right and wrong and what we are and are not allowed to do.

Daddy bought us table games to play with the kids in the neighborhood. This was fun. One of our favorite games was building houses and hotels and taking other people's property, best of all our parents could play with us. It was a lot of fun playing with our parents and friends. Mommy surprised us with a new twist game where we had to stay on dots and twist around our friends. What a laugh, as we loved playing games.

In the evenings, Mommy and Daddy would hug on the couch, and Timmy and I would snuggle up with them. Timmy was always the last one on the couch so he was almost always falling off while I snuggled in tightly. We loved watching late night T.V. shows while we drifted off to sleep in our parents' arms. Sometimes, Timmy ended up on the floor but it was still fun. We felt like we lived in heaven with all our pets, our parents, and our friends. Life was amazing, when all of a sudden it was time to move again.

9 APPLE PICKING

I didn't understand why we were shipped off to Gramma's house again. Was Mommy needing a vacation? Either way, we were going to enjoy Gramma and Grampa's house. Today was strawberry picking day! We went out to a farm and were able to eat and pick as many strawberries as we wanted. The only problem was, after an hour my stomach started hurting so much. I think I overdid it. So, the next day mommy took us apple picking. Wow! There were ladders and so many trees there. Where to start? I didn't know there were so many kinds of apples. Honeycrisp, Red Delicious, McIntosh, and the ones I like best called Northern Spy apples. Mommy let us help her make an apple pie. Timmy was covered in flour and didn't know how to use a rolling pin. Therefore, we had to make apple turnovers so Timmy could participate. We cut up the apples, added cinnamon and brown sugar. Timmy rolled them and then we baked them in the oven. They taste better when you make them at home.

For extra fun after baking gramma let us wash her cupboards in exchange for her milk bottles. We thought we were rich going to the store and buying bubble gum with the milk bottles. I told Timmy to drink more milk so we could get more empty bottles. Since we went through so much milk, Gramma switched our reward to a stick of gum, which was not so great, but still good for helping her with housework. Who knows? Someday, we might have a house and might need to know how to clean it?

Well, I guess our parents did still love us because after a week they were coming to pick us up and take us into our new home. Timmy was so excited he peed his pants, but Gramma did not spank him. She said he was just over-excited! Gramma said our new home was a big school bus that dad painted silver with a bathroom at the back and living room and bedrooms overlooking the roads. What? Our new home was a bus? Yes, that's what Gramma said!

10 THE SILVER BUS

Daddy showed up in the new silver bullet bus with a washroom, bedrooms, living room and a kitchen. We're going on a cross country ride on a big bus. Wow, it was pretty cool living on a bus. Timmy could see his poop fall on the highway from the bathroom toilet as we drove across Ontario looking for our new place to live. Dad would stop and tell us to jump out when we came to a lake to take a bath. Timmy was always thrown in first to test the water temperature. It was fun sleeping in a bunk and looking out the window at the highway, trees and cities going by. I wondered where we would live next? For months we just went from town to town and had fun. All of sudden, Dad stopped the bus and said we had a new home in Sauble Beach close to a jumping jack trampoline shop. Wow, living on a beach in the summer with new friends! We felt like we were in paradise!

My new friend's parents owned a hotel down the road from the beach and had lots of money. This was the life swimming, friends, stores, and lots of people. Life was so much fun we joined a church choir and had costumes for a Christmas play. I wondered if Timmy might become a professional singer? I found a cute stray dog that would follow me to school and home every night. Sometimes we would go on weekends to visit different parks and churches, and the dog would just follow us everywhere without a leash. This dog adopted us! We named him Candy.

11 OUR DOG CANDY

We parked our silver bullet bus outside our new cottage on the beach and ran into the warm water and Timmy dunked his face on the wave. I thought it was time as a big sister to teach Timmy to swim since we lived close to the water and he would need to learn if he wanted to use that big floater in the back.

As Timmy and I approached the beach, I told him he could swim that all children can swim and all he had to do was float and hold his nose tight. Hummm, Timmy sank and was unable to swim and went home crying to Mommy. Oh boy, I thought I was going to get sent to my room again, but instead, Dad was taking us for swimming lessons in the lake to learn to swim with the fishes and the waves! Maybe someday Timmy would become a famous swimmer because with Daddy's help he learned how to swim very quickly.

When daddy sold the farm, we had to leave all our pets behind but now we had Candy the dog who loved Sauble Beach. Candy would walk the beach every day and swim in the lake like a true professional swimmer. Sometimes Timmy would grip onto Candy's head while swimming through the water like she was a dolphin. Everyone thought we had a cool dog.

12 SNUGGLES

Mommy wanted us to have a mini vacation before school started and since we missed our pets from the farm, she took us to visit our cousin Tammy's farm. She had horses, cows and lots of barns. Tammy's mom cooked homemade buns and desserts every day. This reminded me of when we lived on a farm, but Tammy's farm was bigger. We handed out carrots and apples to the horses and hay to the cows. Candy loved Tammy's farm too but I don't think she liked Timmy riding her like a horse out of the water.

Tammy, we and our cousins decided to go down the road on an adventure. We ran into a group of kids that didn't look very nice and didn't say "Hi!" They started to call us names and said we couldn't swim like they could because they lived on a farm up the road. So Tammy, Timmy, and I jumped into a little river under a bridge and started swimming to show them how well Daddy had taught Timmy to swim. All of a sudden, a wave caught me, like some kind of undertow and I couldn't get back up to breathe. I felt my body go limp and I watched as Timmy and Tammy yelled for me to grab a rope that they were trying to throw to me. But I kept going under water and I was really scared and it was hard to breathe.

All of a sudden out of nowhere came Timmy and Candy. They jumped into the water. Timmy grabbed me while holding onto Candy's neck. Timmy had learned to swim now from Daddy and was expertly holding onto Candy's neck and riding her through the waves. They pulled me from the water and put me on Candy's back for a ride back to the farm. Our parents took me to the hospital to get the water pumped out of me. The doctor said I could have died if Timmy hadn't jumped into the water and saved me when he did. The doctors kept me overnight for observation. I felt alone and scared for the first time in a cold hospital room. All of a sudden Daddy popped his head into my room with Timmy and sneaked the little guy under my covers and told me the cure is a brother's love. Out of the corner of my eye, I could see Fuzzy the fly was in the window.

Fuzzy looked like he was trying frantically to get out the window in the hospital, I wondered why he just didn't fly out the door? I fell asleep with my brother snuggling me tightly and telling me how much he loved me.

It must be morning; the bright sun came shining in on our faces and the nurse spoke up and shouted: "What are you doing in here?" My daddy said to the nurse: "Bevy just needed her brother's love last night." Timmy woke up laughing and kissing my face. To my surprise, I was all better and the nurse said I could probably go home. The doctors and nurses rushed into the room and spoke up: "It was a miracle and who was this little boy in bed with this almost drowned child?" "What? (Timmy shouted) I am her little brother and she's coming home today!" Daddy later said Timmy saved my life, and that all I needed was a big hug to make me all better. It was then I realized I had been rewarded with the greatest gift of my life, a little brother, Timmy, whom I could love for the rest of my life!

The end. 😊

Be on the outlook for our next book.

CONCLUSION

I hope you enjoyed reading this book about our childhood adventures. Our father was an inventor so we moved every year and enjoyed a magical childhood. I found when reading this book out loud it was enjoyed by all ages.

Children like reading this adventure book and asking questions while they enter a visionary dream state. This book seems to trigger parents' memories of growing up while reading the stories to their children. Adults like reading the stories and floating down their own memory lane. Teachers like this book for their students as a part of our history while it teaches children to go outside and play instead of staying in the house all day. You never know what adventures await you when you explore our great Canadian outdoors. I hope you enjoyed this book and thank you so much for your purchase. Please feel free to visit my website and send me a personal email on how this book touched you. Thanks again, Beverley Rose Lynn Thomson, BComm aka Bevy!

ABOUT THE ILLUSTRATOR

Debbie Cotton resides with her husband and two sons on Jack Rabbit Run in Ontario. They purchased their home over 7 years ago as a cottage only to completely renovate it resulting in a beautiful stylish lakeside home. Not only does Debbie have a keen eye for interior design, as an instructor of the arts she is a well-known artist in the Decorative Painting Industry. She is an award-winning artist and has been published within the pages of many magazines, an author for instructional acrylic painting books, offers painting kits and videos and has traveled throughout North America to share her painting techniques with hundreds of students. Her warm and inviting personality lean towards a relaxed and informative learning environment. She is an ambassador artist with Royal Brush and a member of DecoArt Americana Helping Artist program. On occasion you can find Debbie teaching paint classes at the local pub in Port Perry. Debbie is now very proud to create these cartoon style illustrations for Beverley's first children's book.

You can find Debbie's designs and zoom classes

@ www.simply-cotton.com

YouTube - Deb Cotton's Paintings Facebook

- Debbie Cotton Facebook

- Deb's Wine & Paint Etsy – SimplyCottonArt

ABOUT THE EDITORS

Pat and her husband Taras moved back to Ontario after teaching for 20 years in Hong Kong to retire in Canada. After fifty years of teaching Pat has written a book called <u>Tips and Tidbits for Parents and Teachers</u>. Both she and her husband were asked to edit this book because of their experience and education. Pat is also a public speaker and singer, and uses music in her education. We thank both Pat and Taras for correcting the grammar, suggesting direction and editing this book. Pat has also participated in authoring a new inspirational book called <u>Empowered in Heels</u> available on Amazon.

ABOUT THE AUTHOR

Beverley's dad was an inventor and her mom a cake decorator and homemaker. She grew up with her brother Tim and traveling parents that like to move every year of her life. In this book Beverley enjoys writing about her childhood adventures with her brother Timmy who lives in Ontario. Not only is it a walk down memory lane, but with times changing so quickly it's a way to reminisce on the way life used to be so simple and free. Beverley's nieces and friends' children love listening to her stories so she thought she would write this book to share their experiences with everyone. She hopes you enjoy this book and it brings back your own memories as you share it with your children.

After working in the corporate world, she decided to open up her own cleaning business after she had a dream. Today she is a web designer, author, speaker, business owner, YouTuber, book designer and free spirit animal lover.

Beverley's best achievement is trademarking and creating https://MaidMart.com a detailed residential and commercial cleaning company that covers the Greater Toronto Area.

Beverley first started writing when her poem Hidden Treasures was published while in university with a group of artists. She is also a co-author for the book Empowered in Heels and proof reader for Empowered in Heels 2 now available on Amazon. Beverley is a contest winner for a short story – Gift of Arts Short Story Contest submission for a children's story submitted on the adventures of Pee Wee & Ginger her two doggies. Her dream is to educate the public on the fair treatment of animals around the world. You can learn more about Beverley on her website: https://BeverleyThomson.com

Manufactured by Amazon.ca
Bolton, ON